Raising Kids With Disabilities

Understanding Differences in Autism, Asperger's, ADHD and How Parents Can Help Children With Disabilities Overcome Challenges to Live a Happier and More Fulfilling Life

Frank Dixon

Before we begin, I have something special waiting for you. An action-packed 1 page printout with a few quick & easy tips taken from this book that you can start using today to become a better parent right now!

It's my gift to you, free of cost. Think of it as my way of saying thank you to you for purchasing this book.

Claim your download of Profoundly Positive Parenting with Frank Dixon by scanning the QR code below and join my mailing list.

Sign up below to grab your free copy, print it out and hang it on the fridge!

Sign Up By Scanning The QR Code With Your Phone's Camera To Be Redirected To A Page To Enter Your Email And Receive INSTANT Access To Your Download

Before we jump in, I'd like to express my gratitude. I know this mustn't be the first book you came across and yet you still decided to give it a read. There are numerous courses and guides you could have picked instead that promise to make you an ideal and well-rounded parent while raising your children to be the best they can be.

But for some reason, mine stood out from the rest and this makes me the happiest person on the planet right now. If you stick with it, I promise this will be a worthwhile read.

In the pages that follow, you're going to learn the best parenting skills so that your child can grow to become the best version of themselves and in doing so experience a meaningful understanding of what it means to be an effective parent.

Notable Quotes About Parenting

"Children Must Be Taught How To Think, Not What To Think."

– Margaret Mead

"It's easier to build strong children than to fix broken men [or women]."

- Frederick Douglass

"Truly great friends are hard to find, difficult to leave, and impossible to forget."

– George Randolf

"Nothing in life is to be feared, it is only to be understood. Now is the time to understand more, so that we may fear less."

– Scientist Marie Curie

Table of Contents

Introduction

It isn't uncommon to hear second- or third-time parents say that they don't recall how they raised their first- or second-born on their own. It is true. Like every pregnancy is different, every child can be different, too. Some are naturally quiet and would sleep for hours in peace—no matter how much noise you make. Some are fussy and would keep you on your toes, demanding that you rock them every minute of the day.

But even more difficult is raising a child with disabilities—the type that doesn't come with any noticeable symptoms or signs. Learning disabilities, for instance, are often diagnosed later when parents realize their child is not reaching the same milestones. Other children, their age, are reaching. Imagine the first few years where they helplessly try everything to understand what's wrong and how they can make life easier for their beloved child.

A disability, no matter in what form, affects a family. It changes the dynamics completely. Parents become bound to pay more attention to the child with a disability, unintentionally neglecting their other children. This can cause resentment and promote sibling rivalry. It affects the mental and emotional well-being of everyone in the house.

Yet a disability doesn't mean the end of the world. It doesn't mean that the child will remain dependent on others. It doesn't mean that you have to provide care and support 24/7. Children with disabilities can lead a successful and fulfilling life, too. They, too, can reach for their dreams and achieve them. They can have meaningful relationships with everyone. They can have prospering careers, follow their passions, find love, get married, and have a family to call their own.

That being said, in this book, we shall look at one specific category of disability—learning disability. Learning disabilities or disorders are umbrella terms for an array of learning problems. A learning disability isn't a problem alone with intelligence or motivation. Children aren't lazy or dumb, as many people and educators assume at first. In most cases, they are exceptionally smart. Their interests lie elsewhere. Their brains are wired differently and, therefore, interpret information differently.

Simply put, children with learning disabilities see, hear, and comprehend things differently. Some may require more time to understand and respond, whereas others do poorly with multiple instructions. This can lead to problems with understanding new information or mastering new skills that they can use. The most common learning disabilities include problems with reading, math, writing, math, communication, or reasoning, etc.

As learning disabilities can look different from one child to another, it can be challenging for parents to diagnose the issue on their own. At first, they may feel that their child lacks interest in some areas of study, like math or English comprehension. For example, they may love listening to storybooks but can't read them. They may love drawing pictures but are not good at math. They may want to share their ideas and thoughts but never find the right words to express themselves. These are all signs of learning disabilities that often get interpreted wrong by educators and parents.

This lack of understanding, combined with the little instruction one receives from doctors and specialists on how to provide care and meet the needs of these children, can lead to extreme family stress. Add to that mix the toxicity from others where they blame the mother for the poor brain development during pregnancy.

The pressure that it puts on parents and siblings should no longer remain an unaddressed issue. We need help from everyone, and the best way to get it is through education. We need to become advocates for our children's special needs and make others aware of the challenges and stress it brings along. We need to tell them to be more considerate and compassionate with their words and actions toward us and our children. We need to become supercharged, exceptional, and self-compassionate so that we can handle taking responsibility for a child with disabilities and ensure that they grow up in a healthy and affectionate environment.

Let this book serve as a guide for you and others who are in the same boat as you. Let this light your path with valuable insights into the world of learning disabilities and prepare you to take on the challenge of successfully raising a child with disabilities.

Chapter 1:

Learning Disabilities: An Unplanned Journey

For most parents, signs of a disability don't show all of a sudden. They may not know that their child has ADHD or Asperger's until they start school. They may then consult a doctor or specialist to find out what could be the reason and be presented with a harsh diagnosis.

Due to the wide variations, it is difficult, even for experts, to identify the disability. It isn't like the symptoms vary in each disability. Profiling thus becomes harder, but once a confirmed diagnosis is received, parents are often met with a setback. Sure, they knew something was wrong, but they weren't always prepared to deal with a disability without a cure. They have little knowledge of its management and treatment options. In the beginning, they have trouble changing the house and routines to ensure management of the symptoms.

Knowing about the different learning disabilities common in children helps you prepare for them. When you know the symptoms, you can catch the disorder earlier. You can then take the necessary steps and seek therapies and alternative treatments to promote healthy development.

This first chapter talks about the three most common learning disorders in children: attention-deficit hyperactivity disorder (ADHD), autism, and Asperger's syndrome. The more we know about the symptoms, risk factors, and causes, the more equipped we can be to make life easier for our children with special needs.

Attention-Deficit Hyperactivity Disorder (ADHD)

Some kids are naturally excitable and energetic. They get hyped over the smallest things. It feels like they never run out of fuel. Nothing they do exhausts them. For parents, tending to such a child may become difficult. We define these children as hyperactive, but the term may be misleading. They just have high spirits and take longer to tire out. Attention-deficit children, on the other hand, are those who face struggles with attention and concentration. They get distracted easily and often complain of having too many distractions around them. Both these conditions can make it difficult for them to grow up as they should.

Although it isn't uncommon for children to struggle with taking instructions, listening, and paying attention, children with ADHD struggle harder and more often. An example would be not having the patience to wait for their turn when told to.

Children with ADHD are:

Inattentive

They get distracted easily and have a challenging time sticking to a single task. Due to their limited processing capacity, they often miss out on important details, cannot take instructions, and cannot finish what they started. Their biggest enemy is procrastination or daydreaming. They dawdle too much. They may appear forgetful, absentminded, and lose track of things.

Inattentive children also make careless mistakes at school. They don't do well with listening and noting down lectures, having long conversations, or reading big paragraphs. They may appear at a loss when spoken to about something because their mind is elsewhere. When given tasks at school or chores at home, they lose focus quickly.

Other signs include problems with organization such as not knowing how to manage time and resources. They often miss deadlines and avoid tasks that require sustained mental efforts like filling forms. They are forgetful and will forget where they kept their books, bag, or eyeglasses.

Hyperactive

They are often fidgety, easily bored, and restless. You may notice them getting anxious easily. They will pace around the room and not sit still or quieten down. They will try to rush through things and make mistakes. Their actions, although unintentionally, disrupt others. The constant jumping, climbing, or craving attention gets others frustrated. Others can easily misinterpret it as misbehavior.

Impulsive

Same is the case with their impulsivity. They act without thinking, react without responding, and interrupt without notice. To seek attention, they may resort to behaviors like pushing or grabbing the person of interest because they can't wait for their turn. This often results in attempting things without permission, like going into someone's bedroom when at a guest's house or using their items without inquiring first. Such acts often land them in hot water and can also be deemed as risky. For example, they may not want to wait for the light to turn green and start walking. When scolded, they can have intense emotional reactions that include screaming, hitting, and lying on the floor.

Some common examples of their hyperactivity and impulsivity include tapping hands and feet; inability to stay seated; being "on the go" always; blurting out answers and suggestions before a question has been finished; cutting between conversations; inability to enjoy leisure things quietly; etc.

Since it is natural for kids to remain distracted, restless, and impatient, it is hard to determine if a child has a serious disorder or is just making up excuses to not study.

Autism

Autism, or autism spectrum disorder (ASD), refers to a broad range of conditions described by challenges with repetitive behaviors, social skills, speech, and communication. One in every forty-four children in the U.S. today is affected, as per statistics from the Centers for Disease Control (CDC, 2018).

Autism has many subtypes. It is most influenced by a series of genetic and environmental factors. Since it can have a wide range of symptoms, every person may experience it differently. They may have a distinct set of strengths and weaknesses. Autism isn't a disability itself. It is just a difference in how the brain interprets things. Think of it as unique wiring in the brain that causes a difference in the way it perceives information and problem-solving. Depending on how much assistance and support one requires, there are five categories of autism ranging from high-functioning to low-functioning. Children with high-functioning autism require minimum to little help with day-to-day tasks. Children with low-functioning seek more dependence and care.

We can spot the first signs of autism at three. Some parents may reckon delays in reaching milestones earlier. The earlier the condition is diagnosed, the sooner appropriate interventions can happen.

People with autism struggle with communication and speech. They have trouble comprehending what others think and say. Unlike other children and adults, they may not decipher emotions or sarcasm correctly. They fear rejection and humiliation from others and therefore have a harder time expressing themselves using words, touch, or facial expressions.

Parents of autistic children also report issues with learning. Their skills develop unevenly. They may outsmart others in certain areas like music, arts, and analytical tests but fail to grasp the basics of other subjects like math, reasoning, memory, etc.

Some other noticeable symptoms include no eye contact, a narrow range of interests; high sensitivity to sounds, lights, and touches; difficulty with self-expression; flat or robotic voice; repetitive actions; etc.

Asperger's Syndrome

Asperger's syndrome was first discovered and identified as a disorder by a Viennese pediatrician, Hans Asperger, in the 1940s. He noticed autism-like symptoms and difficulties in communication and social skills in boys with normal language development and intelligence. For many years, experts believed that Asperger's was a milder form of autism and classified it as a high-functioning type of autism. People would call it having a "hash" of autism. It wasn't until 1994 that Asperger's was classified officially as a separate disorder from autism and added to the American Psychiatric Association's Diagnostic and Statistical Manual of Mental Disorders (DSM-IV). Then, in 2013, the DSM-5 categorized autism, Asperger's, and other pervasive developmental disorders under the umbrella of autism spectrum disorder.

Many parents confuse autism with Asperger's syndrome. Asperger's syndrome is indeed a subtype of autism, but it is also different from it on a lot of levels. The biggest difference lies in the severity of symptoms in autism and their absence or reduction in Asperger's. Children with Asperger's don't experience language delays. They may appear affected mildly at times, but once they find something they are passionate to talk about, they will show you what having exceptional communication and speech skills is like. On a normal day, it will be hard for you to differentiate between a neurotypical child and one with Asperger's syndrome.

Second, children with autism appear uninterested in others and aloof. This isn't the case with those with Asperger's syndrome. Kids with Asperger's syndrome want to fit in with others and interact with them—it's just that they don't know how to. They appear socially awkward to many, don't understand conventional social rules, and have little to no empathy. They have trouble maintaining eye contact and may give the impression of appearing unengaged in conversations.

As stated before, when they find something that interests them, their passion for it borders on obsession. Children with Asperger's like to collect and keep things like stamps, rocks, and ribbons. They have good rote memory skills but fail to understand abstract concepts.

Their speech patterns are also different. They may appear unusual, have a rhythmic nature, appear too formal, or lack inflection. Their voices may be too high-pitched and loud. This happens because they don't understand the subtleties of language, sarcasm, humor, or the irony of it.

Finally, Asperger's differs from autism in terms of cognitive ability. According to its definition, a person with Asperger's can't have a clinically significant cognitive delay. Unlike children with autism, they don't have any intellectual disabilities. Many of them possess average to above-average intelligence.

Signs and Symptoms of Children With a Learning Disability

A lot of misconceptions about disabled children prevail in society. Parents question, "Is a mental illness a disability?" most often because they want to know the amount of care and effort they must guarantee when raising a disabled child. Unlike other mental disorders like obsessive-compulsive disorder (OCD), post-traumatic stress disorder (PTSD), or schizophrenia, learning disabilities don't handicap the child forever. There may not be a guaranteed form of treatment currently, but research and methods that manage its symptoms are equally beneficial. Besides, with early interventions and therapies for speech and communication effectiveness, children with learning disabilities can pick up things like others and become as proficient in language and social skills as other children their age. They may still stumble and need support, but they can lead independent and successful lives on their own.

There are countless famous people that you hear about every day doing incredible, out-of-this-world things despite being on the autism spectrum. People like Bill Gates, Keanu Reeves, Steven Spielberg, Albert Einstein, and Walt Disney are a few names you might want to know about.

As a conclusion to this chapter, let's take a quick recap of the symptoms most commonly observed among children of different ages. Knowing how the symptoms manifest and reveal themselves is the first step to seeking medical help.

Preschool

- Trouble pronouncing words
- Difficulty finding the right word
- Poor coordination
- Difficulty learning alphabets, numbers, shapes, or days of the week
- Trouble following directions or routines
- Difficulty in controlling pencils, colors, scissors, etc.
- Difficulty with tying shoelaces, zippers, and buttons

Ages 5–9

- Difficulty in connecting letters with their sound
- Difficulty with blending sounds to create words
- Trouble with basic math concepts
- Difficulty with learning new skills

- Confusing basic words while reading
- Trouble telling time and remembering its sequences
- Misspelling words and making repetitive blunders

Ages 10–13

- Poor reading, comprehension, and math skills
- Difficulty answering open-ended questions and word problems
- Trouble and hesitance with reading aloud or writing
- Poor organizational skills
- Inability to have classroom discussions
- Difficulty with self-expression
- Spelling same words differently every time

Chapter 2:

Common Challenges for the Family

When someone talks about learning disabilities, the first thought that crosses our minds is that they are talking about someone who can't read or write. A learning disability is more than that. It doesn't imply that the individual with it can't read or write. They can, but they just find it harder. They may struggle with math problems that children their age can solve on their fingers. They also have trouble with organization and paying attention to instructions.

Being their primary caregiver, as parents, we are faced with a unique challenge that not many people understand or experience. It can take a toll on their emotional and mental health. It can cause them to become anxious upon receiving an invitation to a wedding or event where they must take their children along. They may have a challenging time at work and social events where they have to speak about how their child is different and face backlash and stereotyping. Then comes the task of scheduling therapy appointments, doctor's visits, and taking care of other children's needs if any.

Add to that the challenges with diet and nutrition and running a household. Here are the words of Rose Reif, certified rehabilitation counselor, and board-certified to provide telemental health:

> Raising a disabled child can feel a lot like running a marathon. Every time you feel like you are near the finish line, it gets moved further away from you. You also receive no cheers from the crowd for doing great and no one seems interested in your journey or hard work. (Fleming, 2021)

This leads to parents feeling exhausted, frustrated, and overwhelmed most of the time.

There are other emotional and mental challenges parents have to deal with. We shall discuss them in this next chapter and find out more about the day-to-day life of a parent raising a disabled child.

For Parents, the Reality Is Different

Many parents experience guilt as well. They blame themselves for the situation their child is in; others don't leave them at peace. In many religious and conservative homes, elders blame the women for bearing a child with disabilities (Taderera & Hall, 2017). Men blame their wives for bringing children with poor competence into this world. This blaming is nonsensical because they hold no truth. Even today, scientists and medical experts are unsure about how learning disabilities manifest. Surely, some theories indicate a strong genetic link, but there is no concrete evidence to state it as obvious. Therefore, blaming the mother or parents for being irresponsible during pregnancy is pointless. It hurts their sentiments and makes them believe it as truth. This can cause depression, anger, and negative thinking. When one continuously blames themselves for something they haven't done, their mental peace suffers.

Second, there is a lot of stereotyping that parents have to face. In most cases, parents face a lack of understanding from their friends and families regarding the challenges of raising a child with a disability. They often mistake a child's sensory issues as misbehavior and school parents over their poor parenting style. When it comes to social events, parents are requested to not bring their children along, as they feel anxious when loud music is played. Places with the crowd also become inaccessible, as there is unpredictability involved. Children with autism or Asperger's syndrome need structure in their lives. Anything out of the ordinary upsets them. Similarly, when a child has a meltdown in a public setting, parents are met with pity eyes. People don't show empathy toward them and believe that misbehavior is a sign of their weak parenting.

Lack of cooperation from others, especially from educators and teachers, also affects a parent's emotional health. When children come home crying because they were scolded or put into detention for scoring poorly in a test, it hurts a parent the most. Although more and more schools are becoming supportive and active in ensuring additional help for children with special needs, teachers and administration need to become compassionate and understanding. They must ensure a safe and healthy environment for the child where they feel appreciated and important. Ignoring their unique needs puts more pressure on a parent, as they have to fill in one more role. Schools should also initiate programs that cater to a child's specific needs and help them secure a successful and prospering future.

Uncertainty about the future is another important concern and challenge. Parents assume that children with disabilities will require care all their lives. They worry about who will look after them once they are gone. Who will pay for the expenses, clean after them, take care of their medication and routine, etc.? These are genuine concerns that keep many parents awake at night. However, luckily, with learning disabilities, most children don't require as much care as a child with a physical disability would. Children with learning disabilities can take care of themselves in most cases and lead independent, fulfilling, and successful lives.

Another challenge is financing. When parents receive a diagnosis, they also receive many plans and treatment options. In many countries, the government pays for most of the care but not in all areas. If parents wish to adopt better treatment and intervention programs, they have to enroll in them. Those don't come free. If they take children for therapists, have tutors coming in the home to teach children, and have to pay for additional help to look after house chores during weekends, these all become supplementary expenses. In one study, researchers studied the family structure of children with disabilities and found that most of the children with a learning disability are raised by unemployed, single parents who have little support from external sources (Amato et al., 2015). This can add to the financial strain on the parent.

Parents also face the challenge of their children being left out. It is common knowledge that children with special needs have difficulty making friends. Kids with learning disabilities don't have friends due to lack of social and effective communication skills. For a parent, it is no less than a nightmare. They fear that their children will never find people who love and appreciate them and value their importance in their lives. They fear that they won't do well in group settings and struggle with making friends at work, too. The fear of rejection adds to their emotional stress, as they don't want the best for the child.

One simply can't ignore the additional stress it puts on a parent when raising a child with disabilities. In one study, researchers found that mothers of adolescents and adults with autism experience the same levels of stress hormones as soldiers in combat (Diament, 2009). The everyday strain of providing effective care and assistance can easily lead to mental fatigue and exhaustion. It taxes their emotional and physical well-being. It also drains the energy of everyone else in the house because everyone's attention turns to the child with special needs. Parents also worry about the state of their children's mental health. They can only imagine what the child must go through every time they are forced to take part in a discussion, study for a test, and pay attention to the instructions they are given. They also worry if they are doing enough or not.

Guilt is another common challenge that parents face. They feel sad for the limited ability of their child. There is only so much they can do. They feel sad because they can't protect their children all the time. They feel guilty when they see their other children growing up on their own without much attention. Spouses worry that while taking care of the disabled child, they will neglect their partner and drift apart. They also experience jealousy and resentment toward those with "normal" children.

Chapter 3:

Identify How Your Child Learns Best

To encourage learning in children with learning disabilities, the first thing that parents must do is understand how they learn best. We all have different learning styles. Some have a great memory and can recall everything they learned during a lecture or meeting with clarity. Some are more drawn toward visuals and associate images with content. For example, if they are listening to a story about a bear with a horn stuck in its foot, they will create an image of a bear in their head and then learn the content as if watching a movie. Some kids will hum a song about different body parts because that is the only way they can remember. They will do the same with things that involve a sequence like days of the week or the alphabet.

Since children with learning disabilities experience the world in their unique way, knowing about these variations and applying the tools that work best for them is essential. Understanding the different types of learners will also make managing studies easier. It will help them feel more confident and take part in discussions more actively. Without this knowledge, teachers and parents will keep bumping their heads in the wall without any progress whatsoever because their child's unique learning style remains unknown.

Once you know how your child processes new information best, you can adjust your mode of teaching accordingly. This will reduce the amount of time and effort required to get something in their head.

Although there can be more types of learners, there are three major types that we shall discuss in this chapter. The rest are a subpart of these and are often discussed independently.

Visual Learners

Visual learners learn best through pictures and reading words. Sight is their strongest weapon. They understand and remember things by learning in their heads. Creating an image in the mind makes learning easier for them. Visual learners are neat and clean. You may notice them closing their eyes when they hear or read anything. It's because they are trying to visualize the story or associate certain words with their images. Visual learners are easily distracted, though. The magical moment can come to an end if they hear something odd. They also don't do well with spoken directions, especially when multiple colors, shapes, and arts attract them. They also happen to be fond story readers.

During tests, they do well when images accompany questions. If given the choice, they will choose to give exams using visual tools rather than verbally. Visual learners benefit from written content as well. If you want them to remember something, you should present it in the form of charts, maps, and diagrams. For example, if you want to assign them chores in the house, creating a chart with images of what you expect them to do would be ideal. By looking at the picture, they will instantly recall what they are expected to do and perform it without confusion. Visual learners are also good with spellings, as they can memorize the alphabet and its shapes. They love to draw and read from books with pictures.

Auditory Learners

Auditory learners focus more on what they hear or listen to. Learning happens best for them through recalling things they have heard. They store new information by the way it sounds. This means that, unlike visual learners, they are more attentive when instructions are given verbally. They have an easier time recalling than reading written content. Auditory readers read things aloud. If they don't understand a word or sentence, they ask others to read it to them and then memorize its pronunciation. Even when others think they are not paying attention, they are hearing and absorbing everything they say. Auditory learners do best in lecture-based environments, oral exams, and tests. They get excited about classroom discussions and actively take part in them, although this may not be true for someone with a learning disability, as their lack of social skills puts them at a disadvantage. Auditory learners love to sing, perform on stage, and speak different languages.

To promote learning, you can teach lectures by giving them a tune and melody. You can also come up with a chant of your own that serves as an encouragement to read. You can practice learning new words by focusing on the sounds they make. You can listen to audiobooks together while on the move or before bedtime.

Kinesthetic (Tactile) Learner

Tactile learners learn best by touching and doing. Physical movement allows them to understand and remember things. We can call them hands-on learners, too, as they prefer to touch, move, draw, and build what they are learning about. They do well in areas that involve physical activity. Tactile learners use their hands for gestures a lot. Due to excessive movement and their inability to remain seated in peace, they tire out easily and thus require frequent breaks.

Tactile learners get bored easily. They must do something to keep their brain attentive. In school, they would keep moving their hands to focus. They would play with a pencil; empty and refill their stationery box; or keep turning pages of the book. On the bright side, they are exceptionally coordinated and active in sports. If a day involves an activity, they will easily recall it later. However, they will fail to recall what they were wearing or who they were with.

The best way to encourage tactile learning is through physically expressed praise. A hug, pat on the back, or a kiss on the cheek to celebrate good grades or accomplishment of a task goes a long way for them. Tactile learners benefit from hand-on activities, props, skits, lab classes, and field trips. They love sports, dance, martial arts, drama, and arts and crafts that involve creating new things from scratch.

Chapter 4:

Manage Behavior

According to statistics, one in five school-going kids in the U.S. have a learning disability (Understood Team, n.d.). For parents, managing behavior is another elemental concern. It can be confusing to know what the child can do and cannot do. Mostly, children with special needs are smart, know a great deal, and can reason well. However, when it comes to reading or writing, they fail to show results. For example, children with dyslexia often complain of seeing the alphabet dance in front of their eyes. Ask them anything orally, and they will have an answer. Yet, the minute you ask them to write down their answer, they can't. Educators and parents assume that they are disinterested in the subject and are told to try harder. However, let's be clear about one thing: They are trying their best. They don't want to disappoint you either. They aren't being lazy or purposely dumb. They aren't making excuses as to why they can't read or write but know about everything verbally. It is the reality they live with. Until we provide help with their speech and writing, they can't do as well as their peers.

Another confusion that parents face is the large hiatus between what the child can't do and won't do. For parents with an autistic child, it can become vexing when they can't control the child's actions. They can't know if they should continue to push forward or reduce their expectations from them. This is where they need to shift their focus from what the child can't do to why the child won't do it. Perhaps teaching methods aren't appropriate. Perhaps your lack of patience affects the child's emotional state, or it could be the lack of trust in their abilities that leads to poor self-esteem and misbehavior in them.

This confusion between a child's inability to do something and misbehavior is a common one. Some children indeed find it easier to give up than try when they come across a task that is too demanding. This means that when your child tells you they hate doing something, it could be because they find it too challenging. They aren't always trying to misbehave.

Misbehavior is a challenge for parents. When children don't find the right outlets for self-expression, are looked down upon, and are not provided the type of care and help they require getting over their weaknesses, they can act out. When it starts to happen daily, it can frustrate parents, too. It can be anxiety-provoking for them. Parents must, therefore, look for strategies that will prevent misbehavior from the get-go; they must come up with strategies that limit misbehavior as well as rely on their gut to know how long their child lasts at a party or restaurant before exploding.

Parents must try to work out what works best, what doesn't, what leads to frustration, and what brings their child happiness. They must analyze and think carefully about practices that help manage behavior in the house and outside.

Common Challenges for Disabled Children

As parents, you should know that a child rarely acts out for fun. There is always an unmet need that triggers frustration and anger in them. Learning disabilities affect their behavior. Imagine how helpless and vulnerable you will feel when surrounded by people with better intellect and more wisdom than you. You will forever feel like the underdog, just trying your best to appear smart. Now, imagine having to live your life every day like this. Would you not be frustrated?

Children with learning disabilities go through something similar every day. They have to prove that they are equally competent as their peers. However, when they fail to prove their expertise, it leads to the buildup of negative emotions in them. There comes a point when they stop trying altogether because they see no point in it. Their lack of confidence in their ability to learn and improve their communication and social skills makes them bitter. They make excuses to cover up for their shortcomings. This can make improvement difficult.

In one study, researchers found that children with learning disabilities experience behavior problems connected to poor self-confidence and anxiety (Diakakis et al., 2008). One common symptom is aggressiveness. They are likelier to lose temper and have a meltdown than children without a learning disability.

Frustration

Young children and teenagers with learning disabilities are prone to exhibit contradictory patterns of performance and confusion. They struggle with certain tasks but perform others with great accuracy and perfection. For instance, a child may love bedtime stories but behave inappropriately when placed in a reading group with peers. A child may get overly excited over a favorite topic and disrupt the whole class. This may end with their removal from the class and detention.

Frustration is a given in these cases. Children with learning disabilities fail to do well despite being intelligent. It's their lack of ability to mingle and express themselves that puts them behind. They feel frustrated because, like every other child, they want to prove themselves. They want to show the world that they are competent, too.

Bullying

Children with learning disabilities are subjected to bullying and harassment at the hands of their peers and seniors. They are belittled and mocked for their lack of social and communication skills. Upon receiving poor grades or being scolded for showing a lack of interest and attention in class, their classmates often make them the victim of bullying. The bullying doesn't just end there. When they meet other children their age at social parties, they are looked down upon by others.

On the other hand, some children with a learning disability may become a bully and harass others to cover for their shortcomings. This can also be viewed as a coping mechanism. When they victimize others, they feel more in control. They feel powerful and no longer someone with special needs.

Low Self-Esteem

Learning disabilities don't affect a child's behavior and learning; it also impacts their self-esteem (Alesi et al., 2012). They may lose confidence when always ridiculed for the things they can't do. Their lack of self-esteem makes them more vulnerable at the hands of others. They may face difficulty reaching out to their peers for help. They may not be equipped to handle peer pressure and have trouble interacting with their classmates and teachers. Their inability to decipher social cues also affects how they view themselves.

Social Isolation

Lastly, social isolation is another common issue. When children with learning disabilities are constantly called stupid or losers, they begin to isolate themselves from others. Other children feel that they should not hang out with or make friends with someone with poor grades. Children with special needs also lose confidence in their strengths and believe what others tell them. Even when they succeed at something, they attribute it to their luck rather than hard work.

Minimizing Disobedience

Since behavior management is a common outcome caused by frustration, social isolation, and bullying, teaching children how to respond instead of reacting is crucial. By minimizing disobedience, children with a disability can become more patient, tolerant, and appreciative of others and themselves. When they allow themselves to remain calm and not lose their cool in social situations, they can learn ways to be more expressive of how they feel. For example, if they don't understand social cues well, instead of allowing frustration and anger to take over, they can ask the speaker to be clearer. This way, the speaker won't feel disrespected either.

The following piece of advice comes from Sally L. Smith, an American educator who founded a school for children with learning disabilities in 1967. Sally believed that children with learning disabilities had the same strengths and weaknesses as other neurotypical children. She thought disabled children required just a tad bit more attention, care, and help. In an article, she talked about the following points regarding misbehavior in children with ADHD and other learning disorders (Smith, 2002):

Give Them Time and Space

Space and time are organizational tools. We use them to address every task and track performance in every aspect of our lives. It so happens that many children with learning disabilities struggle with organization such as being unable to keep their room clean, not following instructions, and failing to accomplish simple tasks in a designated time window. This shows that they can't link the concepts of time and space efficiently.

Some children have trouble with sequences such as not being able to remember days of the week, alphabetical order, or what task comes first. This leads to trouble with starting new projects, performing, and finishing them.

This is where developing structure and routine comes in. Reinforcing routines can structure time. It allows the breaking of bigger tasks into manageable ones. Routines also help the prevention of tantrums and misbehavior, as there is a degree of predictability involved. Expectations are clear, which prevents frustration and confusion.

Engage in Planning

Similar to providing structure, planning for events, gatherings, and trips also makes it easier for parents to curb inappropriate behavior. Asking them to help plan activities, routines, chores, and events gives children a sense of importance and empowerment. They feel like they are in control of the situation. Asking for their opinions also gives them a chance to be expressive and share their ideas confidently. Involve them in making lists, shopping, and charting tasks and chores, if possible.

Role-Play

We can teach children who panic in social situations how to respond to them via role-play. Parents can turn this exercise into a game where they use flash cards to pick out a social situation or conversation and then play along on how they would react and converse. For instance, if you have planned an upcoming birthday party, everyone will bring gifts for your child, and they will have to say, "Thank you very much." You can practice with them by role-playing different relatives and teaching them how to confidently respond. You can use this approach in many other situations, like role-play on the first day of school after a summer break. Teaching them beforehand how to manage social situations can prevent anxiety and frustration. It will make them feel more confident and improve their self-worth.

Coach About Social Cues

Children with autism, Asperger's syndrome, and ADHD have difficulty reading social signals. Unlike you, they may not successfully decipher someone's facial expressions, a change in the tone of their voice, body language, and gestures. Most children are literate and concrete. They don't deal with nuances, inferences, subtleties, and multiple meanings. When they feel they are being mocked or ridiculed, they lose their cool. As their parent, you can help them read faces, movements, and gestures better. You can coach them on different facial expressions and what emotions they depict. For instance, a frown may indicate displeasure, sadness, or worry. Wide eyes may represent surprise, shock, or excitement. Once they know how the other person feels, they can devise their responses better and have meaningful conversations.

Praise and Admire

Teaching children with disabilities to appreciate their unique talents and strengths is another way to minimize acting out. Train them to be positive about themselves by being grateful for the countless blessings they have. Shift their focus from viewing themselves as abnormal and turn them into an optimistic person. Be sure to offer timely praise and appreciation when you catch them doing something well so that they feel validated. Doing so will naturally make them more inclined to stick with good actions. Make way for small celebrations when they accomplish a goal so that they know that hard work and dedication never go unrewarded. Make your praise sound genuine and specific, so they know exactly what behavior or action is being appreciated.

Chapter 5:

Become a Peaceful Warrior

Parenting special needs children requires fighting—first with yourself, then with your child, and then the world. There is so much that lies on our shoulders. First, we have to gather our spirits and give our children a life that they deserve, minus the pity and sympathy. This is possible when we stop viewing them as disabled. We need to realize that it is our love and attention they crave—not our guilt and anger. Then, we need to pull them up every time they come home crying because no one would be friends with them. We need to remind them that they are not at fault here. We need to reassure that there are good people in the world, too—people who would see *them* and not their disability.

Then comes the toughest battle—the fight we must fight with the world. Sadly, this world and its people are not equipped to handle children with special needs. They feel like they must maintain a safe distance from someone with special needs, both emotionally and physically. They fear they might do something that would trigger a meltdown. They forget that children with learning disabilities aren't any less intelligent. They can sense the hesitance and awkwardness. They can see the pity in your eyes and how you view them.

Therefore, we need to take care of the world and not let our kids feel belittled. It is on us to fill our tanks with exceptional compassion. In doing all this, we become peaceful warriors. We pick our battles wisely. We understand that there is some behavior that we can control and prevent and some that we can't. We understand that there are subjects we must never argue about with our children because it triggers bad emotions, so we tread lightly around them, hoping that they won't read our minds and realize how emotionally tense and empathetic we are.

As soon as you learn to control your emotions and actions around your child, you realize you have the power to change the way others treat your child, too. You can become an advocate for them and their unique disability and educate others about it. You can also get in touch with your child's secondary caregivers and ensure that they are doing their best for your child.

Becoming an Advocate for Your Child

An advocate is someone that defends another person's rights, interests, and needs. It involves promoting and educating others on behalf of those who can't voice their concerns themselves. As an advocate for your kid with special needs, you must become well-informed, have all the knowledge about how to use that information, attend meetings with educators and therapists, and bring to light the concerns you and your child have regarding their progress.

Children with learning disabilities find it difficult to be open about what concerns them. They struggle with expressing their weaknesses. Since a parent knows their child better than anyone, no one can make for a better advocate than them. Unlike their educators and doctors, you have been involved with them since birth. You are most likely to stick around until the end, ensuring that your child's needs are taken care of.

Since you play an important part in all the planning, let's go over how you, as a parent, can become an excellent advocate for your child.

Know the Rules

When you are raising a child with special needs, the school you enroll your child in has to abide by certain laws and regulations. These laws offer children with learning disabilities special services. However, there are eligibility criteria that vary from state to state. Therefore, the first step is to know about these laws and regulations so that you can hold the school accountable if they fail to follow them. In this regard, you can contact the state and seek clarification or contact your local school district office.

Get in Touch With Important People

There are going to be many people who work with your child with special needs directly. These will be their educators and administrators. Know who these people are in both formal and casual settings. If your child is receiving therapy or a special speech-improving program, get to know the therapist and doctors working with them. To remain more engaged, actively take part in school programs and events. Volunteer in the classroom and help school committees to organize functions. If your child shows concern about a certain teacher, take it up with the district office and see if some new arrangement can be done. As a parent, you have every right to demand what's best for your child. Don't hold back, as these are the most crucial years of their life; most of the learning happens around this time as well.

It's Going to Take Some Time

Advocating for your child is going to take time. You need to be solid on your research about the disability; be prompt and available for meeting times; and openly communicate your concerns. You will have to go to meetings, be called in multiple times, and be asked to show proof at different points, so make sure you are ready for it, both emotionally and physically.

Know Your Child's Strengths

Children with learning disabilities aren't dumb. They may be weak in some areas but exceptionally talented in others. Bring those areas to light with the professionals so that they can use the knowledge to connect better with the child. They can use them as tools to strengthen the areas that need work. Also, when positives are highlighted more, it makes the child feel more confident. It also makes it easier to break the ice with a child that finds initiating conversations hard. It also makes the child think that people see the good in them, too.

Ask Questions

Many parents fear asking questions. They don't want to appear nosy and impatient. They think that if they ask a professional too many questions, they will get frustrated and take it out on their child. This is never the case. Asking questions gives you an insight into what's going on in your child's life, how they are responding to the mode of treatment, and what parents can do to improve their condition. Asking questions doesn't imply that you don't know anything about their condition. You are just trying to be an informed parent.

Educate Others

Finally, take out the time to educate others about your child's condition to make it easier for them and others as well. Others will feel more informed and prepared on how to converse with a special needs child. Your research will also help parents going through something similar feel like they aren't the only ones. It will also help shed more light on the disability and help people become more aware and compassionate.

Chapter 6:

Encourage Social Competence

Sadly, the consequences of learning disabilities aren't confined to school. Children with a learning disability face trouble with forming meaningful relationships as well. They need assistance with nonacademic functioning, too, such as taking part in sports or drama. As a result, their self-esteem and confidence take a hit. When we talk about social competence, we talk about interpersonal skills. These include knowledge of both verbal and nonverbal behaviors that we value in social relationships.

Children with a learning disability are less observant of their social environment. They misinterpret social cues and behaviors. They also exhibit immaturity and social ineptness because of their disability. Their need for approval and validation from others causes them to try too hard in unsuitable ways. This makes them less likely to form strong bonds with their peers, educators, and even siblings.

Every social interaction has three elements to call it a successful exchange.

Social Intake: This includes making small talk, comprehending, and taking note of the speaker's saying, their body language, voice emphasis, eye contact, and cultural-specific behavior. Children with a learning disability don't pick on spoken and unspoken cues; misread moods; and don't understand the meanings of others, so they fail to make small talk successful.

Internal Process: For a successful social interaction, both parties must identify and manage their reactions and emotions. Children with learning disabilities miss out on another person's interpretation and work. They misjudge information incorrectly. They don't take into account the emotions and facial expressions of others, leading to inappropriate conclusions and reactions.

Social Output: Social output involves reacting and responding. Once an individual has successfully interpreted the body language, facial expression, and tone of voice, they develop an appropriate response. A child with a learning disability might not craft an appropriate response. They may giggle nervously, provide irrelevant answers, or become emotionally triggered.

Without these three elements, a successful social dialogue ceases to happen.

How Learning Social Skills Can Help Children

The degree and impact of the lack of social skills in a child with a learning disability differs from individual to individual. Some children are more competent when it comes to having conversations. Take Bill Gates, for example. A common man would never conclude that he has a functioning disorder. Bill Gates is reported to have suffered from dyslexia at the age of 20 (Wilson, 2021). Even today, he faces issues with his flat-pitch tone; poor assessment of sarcasm and jokes; and finding suitable words to explain their thoughts and ideas. Albert Einstein suffered something similar in his life, and look at what he achieved. His competence and abilities were different from Bill Gates. The point is that even a common learning disability such as ADHD may show different symptoms in different individuals. Some may experience mild symptoms and need only little assistance, whereas others experience intense symptoms and need complete assistance for everyday functioning.

Developing social competence, however, is beneficial for all children with special needs. It empowers them to speak their mind, fulfill their basic needs, and develop devoted relationships. It encourages them to take part in conversations more actively and be of help to others. In work settings, social skills help employees work on their unique ideas and benefit their organization by bringing them forth and implementing them.

Having the ability to carry themselves gracefully in social settings also helps individuals with learning disabilities feel confident. They can stop viewing themselves as victims or incompetent. When they can manage their symptoms, they can understand jokes, find the right words for self-expression, and read social cues correctly. With the right strategies, practices, and tools, children and adults with learning disabilities can remember things and be of value to others by sharing their experiences and expertise.

They can also control their impulse to interrupt during conversations, which is a common symptom in children with ADHD. With social skills learning, they can become observant about one's body language, gestures, and facial expressions, decoding their internal situation. They can also prevent their mind from wandering around and remain calm and gathered in their thoughts.

Managing Public Outings

For most parents, social gatherings and public spaces are torture. Every time an invitation arrives that calls for the whole family, there is more worry than happiness in the house. You know what's going to happen next. You need to prepare your child in advance on how to carry themselves. You need to talk to them about what's appropriate behavior and what isn't when playing with other children. You need to remind them to not have a meltdown when someone doesn't share something with them. You need to remind them to wait for their turn patiently, be confident when speaking with others, and be considerate of their actions and reactions. You have to school them like this before every event, but you also know what happens when you don't. Unpredictability and change scare them. It causes them to act out in unhealthy ways, making them a laughing stock among other children. Your heart goes out to them, but there is only so much that you can do for them.

Besides, you can't keep them hidden from the world for the rest of their lives. They must learn to regulate their emotions on their own. They must learn to interpret social cues better so that they can have insightful conversations with others confidently. There are various ways to prepare, handle, and teach children how to act in public outings.

Go out during off-peak hours so that you can avoid being stuck in traffic. This is recommended for parents whose children suffer from sensory processing issues. Picking off-peak hours will make it more enjoyable for your family, as there will be fewer distractions. This also applies to visiting restaurants, malls, zoos, parks, and other public places. Research times where there are fewer people so that children can enjoy being where they are without feeling overwhelmed by the crowds.

Choose to go out with your spouse. Having another adult with you will reduce stress and worry on your part. In case something goes wrong, you won't be the only one dealing with it. A partner will help take care of you and your child.

Talk to your child about an event before its actual date. This way, you can mentally prepare them to be in a social space with others. If possible, read them stories about how to behave appropriately and what's expected of them. For example, if you plan to take them grocery shopping with you the coming weekend, look up pictures of what the grocery store would look like, what you will be buying, how much time will you be spending, and who will you be speaking with once there (cashier, salesperson, or other parents). The same goes for when you have the vaccination at the doctor's clinic coming up. Teaching them what to expect will relieve some of their stress and worry. It will also make it a predictable trip for them—as long as things go as planned.

If your child is particular about what they eat, let them pack alongside you when you make their lunch or dinner. Children with ADHD and autism are particular about their dietary needs. Not receiving their expected food item may trigger a meltdown. Also, you won't have to worry about any allergies when you bring packed food from your house.

Think ahead on how you are going to handle a meltdown or tantrum in case it happens. Think about how you will respond to stares and rude comments from strangers because, chances are, as soon as your child starts to act out, all eyes go on you. People judge your parenting style and pass pitiful stares. It can be heartbreaking and stressful. However, you have to take care of your child first. You can ignore the stares and comments and think about them later. In the meantime, you must think about how you are going to end the meltdown and focus on that.

Keep a bag of tricks with you when going to places where your child will be made to wait. Children with learning disabilities tend to get restless and bored easily. They need to have something going on most of the time. Sitting idle or in peace isn't something you would expect from an autistic or hyperactive child. Therefore, to keep them engaged, pack some fun things that entertain and calm them down. These can be toys that they like to hold when they are fidgety, an app on your phone that they can play with, or a book they can read to pass time. In case things get out of control, you can play some soft tunes on your phone and place headphones on them to reduce external noise and distractions.

Chapter 7:

Prepare for Life Success

When we were young, we were told by our parents and teachers that if we did well in school, we would be successful. If we got good grades, graduated with a high GPA, and had certification glorifying our extracurricular activities, we will have it all. Doing well at school felt like the ultimate security. It may have worked for our parents and their parents, but if we look at how fast the world is changing today, we realize that this advice is nothing but bogus.

Our GPA doesn't determine our skill set. Our good grades don't guarantee a great personality. Our awards and certifications don't warrant excellent employee skills. What does matter is our personality, confidence, and ability to put forth great ideas.

Success, today, has a different definition. To some people, it may still be the same (financial wealth). But, to most, it extends to beyond our report cards. For children with special needs, the definition is even more byzantine. As parents, we are told that our children may never fulfill their dreams, get their dream job, and roll in money. We are told that they may never fall in love, find companionship, or have satisfying relationships.

We are reminded of how different they are from others and never compete with other children in academics.

Untrue!

First, success at school doesn't mean success in life. Had this been the case, we wouldn't have billionaires, great innovators, and trailblazing entrepreneurs who changed the course of the world be college dropouts. It proves that success in academics doesn't guarantee success in life.

Success at School Isn't Success in Life

Do you remember all the people you studied with? Try to remember the ones that got straight As in every class and graduated with the highest GPA. Look at their lives and careers now. Did all of them make it big? Are all living the lives of their dreams, going on exotic vacations every year, cruising open waters, and driving big cars?

Did all the good children who were disciplined and submitted their assignments on time make money off of it? Maybe some of them did but not all. This proves that getting all As doesn't guarantee success. True, the school does help in familiarizing us with the basics of the language, math, physical education, and world history, but they fail to teach us basic life skills. To be successful in life, we must indulge and pursue things that keep our interest in life. We must have the patience to keep trying, perseverance to keep moving forward, and self-confidence to accept who we are.

Schools don't teach us what we need. They just ask us to graze along like other sheep in the herd. They don't tell you why you are learning a particular subject or topic and what use it will be. Instead, they ask us to be obedient and follow the rules made by them without question. There is little room for creativity and originality.

To succeed in life, the first thing you are expected to do is step out of your comfort zone, unlearn all that you have learned, and bring your creativity to the forefront. You are expected to think outside the box and not follow the steps of others blindly. You are expected to create a work-life balance and make time for your loved ones as well.

A high school diploma will indeed land you better prospects; it is your personality, willingness to work together as a team player, and innovation that will set you apart. People who dropped out of school or failed didn't end up failing in life. People like Jim Carrey, Oprah Winfrey, and Sir Richard Branson are prime examples of people who never completed school yet are living highly successful lives.

Succeeding at Life: The Ultimate Hack

The following are the most important life skills that you must focus on with your children with special needs. This is the key to succeeding in life, which should be the ultimate goal. These skills have been identified as the most important during a 20-year study involving children with learning disabilities (Raskind & Goldberg, 2003). Developing these skills in your children will give them a huge advantage in life.

Self-Awareness: For children with learning disabilities, knowing their strengths and weaknesses is important. Only then can they work on them. Working on their strengths will increase their confidence. Ask your child to create a list of their strengths and weaknesses. Once they have a list, discuss how they can turn their weaknesses into their strengths. Talk about how they can overcome challenges with strategies that work best for them. For example, if they list communication as a weakness, you can take up speech and communication improvement programs and role-play different social situations where they feel stuck. To boost their self-confidence, encourage them to follow their passions and strengths.

Stress Management: Children with learning disabilities must know how to regulate stress and remain calm. This way, they can overcome social challenges better. Teach them to use words to express their feelings. Teach them how they can express how they feel using a feelings chart. Help them to recognize when they are feeling stressed. Show them better coping strategies when you catch them in a stressful situation. Encourage them to write down their thoughts and feelings and take part in activities that are known to reduce the production of serotonin—the stress hormone in the body. Finally, discuss situations that stress out your child and break it down into smaller scenarios to talk about when they feel the most stressed.

Goal-Setting: Goal-setting involves setting attainable and realistic goals. Goal-setting also involves flexibility and adaptability, as goals often require changing. Children with learning disabilities must be taught to create short-term and long-term goals. They can write them down and create a road map of how they plan to achieve them. If they need to enroll in any special classes or hire a tutor for practicing, be sure to provide them with that. Track their progress and make time to celebrate small wins. In case they fail, don't let them lose heart. Share your own stories about failures and how you overcame them.

Chapter 8:

Don't Forget Self-Care

Self-care should be an important part of our daily lives—even more so for parents raising disabled kids. Self-care allows for some relaxation for the mind, soul, and body. It helps foster well-being and happiness. Emotional well-being always gets linked with self-care practices. Engaging in activities that enhance mood and uplift one's spirits is a blessing. Meditation, exercise, yoga, or just spending some alone time with yourself are all practices that put one in a good mood, clear the mind, and make way for positive thoughts.

Parents of disabled children need more than just run-of-the-mill self-care. They need radical, supercharged, and exceptional compassion. Finding a few moments of seclusion and appreciating the present is like winning the self-care lottery. Since their lives are filled with exceptionalities, they need more care and pampering.

In this final chapter of the book, we shall look at how parents can work on their well-being and become the best caretaker for their children with disabilities. You must remember that to take care of them, nourish them, and fill their lives with happiness and love, you need to fill your soul with the same. You must take care of your needs first so that you may be of help to them.

Your Mental Well-Being Comes First

Your mental health will take a toll when you receive a confirmed diagnosis about your child's disability. You already had a hunch, but there was still hope that you could be wrong. However, the results change everything, and every little fear you had just becomes your reality. You are trapped in the "How, what, and whys" of things. The first thing you say is, "Could it be my fault?"

Once you are past the stage of blaming and guilt, you move toward despair and sadness. You feel like there is nothing you can do to change the diagnosis and that your child is doomed for life. After that comes a sudden surge of positivity where you realize there is still room for improvement.

Once you reach that stage and become open to suggestions, research, and improvement, get all the help you can get. Talk to your child's therapists, educators, school district office, relatives, and friends who have experienced anything remotely similar and listen to their advice. Don't allow your brain to breed negative thoughts. Don't let your spirits go weak.

On days when you feel like giving up, reach out. Find a strong support system. You don't have to do it all alone. When you reach out and connect with people who are walking the same path together, you can come across many coping strategies and resources that will offer a deeper insight. You will instantly feel better just to have someone battling the same with you. You will thank them for understanding what you are going through. Soon, the frustration and anger you first felt will start to disappear. You will no longer feel burdened by your child's extra challenges.

Second, if you need some time alone to gather your thoughts and reenergize, don't fear looking into respite care. Many trained professionals will provide caretaking services to your child. They are trained to talk, bathe, dress, and feed those who need help. Respite care is a short-term break for primary caregivers. It can be arranged for an hour, a day, or even a week, depending on how much time you need to revitalize and take over.

Think of respite care as wanting to refill your pitcher. If you keep using the water in it, without filling it again, you will only run out of water. You can only offer others to drink from it once you have enough for them. You will be of no use to anyone if you are empty. Therefore, take out some time for yourself from your busy routine every week, if not every day. Use that time to do something that you love. It could be pursuing an interest like music, baking a cake from scratch, going for a drive, or reading a book in a quiet place.

If possible, spare five minutes every day for yourself and just yourself. Do something that relaxes you like sipping on coffee, dancing, watching a stand-up routine, or just sitting and gazing out of the window.

You Are Doing GREAT!

No matter what anyone says, know that you are doing your best. Sooner or later, your child is going to appreciate all that you did for them and continue to do. No one can replace you or take care of them better than you. Don't let the judgment of others make you weak. Don't let their opinions overshadow yours. Only you know what's best for your child. Avoid getting into power struggles with your child based on what someone told you to do. Rely only on the wisdom and expertise of medical experts, your child's therapists, or the intervention program in charge.

Stay informed and educate others as well. Don't feel shy asking for help from others. It takes a village to raise a child, so don't isolate yourself from your friends and family. Also, make sure to carve out time for yourself. You shouldn't have to feel guilty about going away from your child for a bit. You have a life of your own. If you have a partner, let their needs not go unnoticed either. Rely on their emotional support. Surround yourself with positive people and thoughts. Your child's disability doesn't limit their options. They too can succeed and lead a happy and fulfilling life.

Don't let anyone tell you otherwise.

Conclusion

Thankfully, we have a dedicated lot of scientists and experts making great strides in understanding how the brain works. This comprehension will pave way for many more, successful interventions and therapies for children with learning disabilities. One such discovery is neuroplasticity. According to experts, neuroplasticity allows for the creation of new neural pathways that help children learn new skills, develop new habits, and better comprehend thoughts. It applies various technologies and methods to access different parts of the brain that require cognitive strengthening.

For children with autism, ADHD, or Asperger's syndrome, neuroplasticity works in two ways. First, it explains how past experiences affect learning disabilities. New research suggests that learning disorders have a genetic component, but it is the wrong stimulation that intensifies it. A history of abuse or punishing a child to perform a standard task worsens their disability and increases fear.

Second, neuroplasticity is also an effective response to learning disorders. You must note that children with learning disabilities don't lack intelligence or a desire to learn. Their brain is wired differently which prevents them from processing information the same way a neurotypical child does. With neuroplasticity, children can change their brain structure, making their learning disability barely noticeable. This is possible when we actively target the regions that require development and strengthening. This way, the brain builds new trails and leads to the desired destination.

Innovative programs promoting the use of strategic brain exercises can help children overcome their learning disability, given that it is not a major disability. For example, children who can't distinguish between different sounds in a word can use computer-based learning programs that slow down the sounds for better comprehension. Regular practice will gradually increase their speed of comprehension.

Further research will hopefully lead to many additional new treatments that combat specific learning disabilities and get to the core of the problem. Until then, we can rely on the strategies and ideas shared in the book and do our best to ensure that our children with special needs lead happy and successful lives.

The goal of the book has been to encourage parents to not view the disability as a roadblock. A diagnosis isn't the end of the world for them. It doesn't prove that they are incompetent. It doesn't suggest that they will forever need assistance. It simply tells you that they will require some more love, attention, and time.

Keep things in perspective. A learning disability isn't insurmountable. Remind yourself that everyone faces obstacles. It's up to you as a parent to teach your child how to deal with those obstacles without becoming discouraged or overwhelmed. Don't let the tests, school bureaucracy, and endless paperwork distract you from what's important—giving your child plenty of emotional and moral support.

Thank you for giving this book a read. I hope you loved reading it as much as I enjoyed writing it. It would make me the happiest person on earth if you would take a moment to leave an honest review. All you have to do is visit the site where you purchased this book: It's that simple! The review doesn't have to be a full-fledged paragraph; a few words will do. Your few words will help others decide if this is what they should be reading as well. Thank you in advance, and best of luck with your parenting adventures. Every moment is a joyous one with a child.

References

ADHD. (n.d.). CAMHS. Retrieved December 25, 2021, from https://www.camhsnorthderbyshire.nhs.uk/learning-disabilities-adhd

Alesi, M., Rappo, G., & Pepi, A. (2012). Self-Esteem at school and self-handicapping in childhood: Comparison of groups with learning disabilities. *Psychological Reports*, *111*(3), 952–962. https://doi.org/10.2466/15.10.pr0.111.6.952-962

Amato, P. R., Patterson, S., & Beattie, B. (2015). Single-parent households and children's educational achievement: A state-level analysis. *Social science research*, *53*, 191–202. https://doi.org/10.1016/j.ssresearch.2015.05.012

Ambrozich, A. (2015). *Survival tips for special needs parents.* The Center for Parenting Education. https://centerforparentingeducation.org/library-of-articles/focus-parents/survival-tips-for-special-needs-parents-youre-not-alone-i-promise/

Autism Society. (2019). *Asperger's syndrome - autism society.* Autism Society. https://www.autism-society.org/what-is/aspergers-syndrome/

Autism Speaks. (2021). *What is autism?* Autism Speaks. https://www.autismspeaks.org/what-autism

CDC. (2018, November 15). *Autism and developmental disabilities monitoring (ADDM) network.* Centers for Disease Control and Prevention. https://www.cdc.gov/ncbddd/autism/addm.html

Challenges faced by special needs families. (2016, June 16). Alabama Family Trust. https://www.alabamafamilytrust.com/challenges-faced-special-needs-families/

Chui, A. (2017, March 10). *Why people who succeed at school don't always succeed in life.* Lifehack; Lifehack. https://www.lifehack.org/560957/success-school-doesnt-equal-success-life

Commission, H. and H. S. (n.d.). *Parenting children with disabilities | navigate life texas.* Www.navigatelifetexas.org. https://www.navigatelifetexas.org/en/family-support/parenting-children-with-disabilities

Diakakis, P., Gardelis, J., Ventouri, K., Nikolaou, K., Koltsida, G., Tsitoura, S., & Constantopoulos, A. (2008). Behavioral problems in children with learning difficulties according to their parents and teachers. *Pediatrics*, *121*(Supplement 2), S100.2-S101. https://doi.org/10.1542/peds.2007-2022cc

Diament, M. (2009, November 10). *Autism Moms Have Stress Similar To Combat Soldiers*. Disability Scoop. https://www.disabilityscoop.com/2009/11/10/autism-moms-stress/6121/

Disabilities - impact of disabilities on families. (2019). Jrank.org. https://family.jrank.org/pages/396/Disabilities-Impact-Disabilities-on-Families.html

Education Planner. (2019). *What's your learning style? The learning styles*. Educationplanner.org. http://www.educationplanner.org/students/self-assessments/learning-styles-styles.shtml

Fleming, L. (2021, July 23). *Support for parenting a child with disabilities*. Verywell Family. https://www.verywellfamily.com/support-for-parenting-a-child-with-disabilities-5192788

Haddad, D. (2019). *Children with learning disabilities can also have behavior problems*. Verywell Family. https://www.verywellfamily.com/how-learning-disabilities-can-affect-behavior-2161916

Hasan, S. (Ed.). (2018). *ADHD (for parents)*. Kidshealth.org. https://kidshealth.org/en/parents/adhd.html

How parents can be advocates for their children. (2013, April 24). Reading Rockets. https://www.readingrockets.org/article/how-parents-can-be-advocates-their-children

Kemp, G., Smith, M., & Segal, J. (2019a, March 12). *Learning disabilities and disorders.* HelpGuide.org. https://www.helpguide.org/articles/autism-learning-disabilities/learning-disabilities-and-disorders.htm

Kemp, G., Smith, M., & Segal, J. (2019b, March 20). *Helping children with learning disabilities.* HelpGuide.org. https://www.helpguide.org/articles/autism-learning-disabilities/helping-children-with-learning-disabilities.htm

Learning disabilities in children can be A challenge at home & school. (n.d.). Child Development Institute. Retrieved December 25, 2021, from https://childdevelopmentinfo.com/learning/learning_disabilities/#gs.kcx5by

Malvik, C. (2020, August 17). *4 types of learning styles: How to accommodate a diverse group of students | rasmussen college.* Rasmussen.edu. https://www.rasmussen.edu/degrees/education/blog/types-of-learning-styles/

Miller, C. (2016, June 7). *Social challenges of kids with learning problems.* Child Mind Institute; Child Mind Institute.

https://childmind.org/article/social-challenges-kids-learning-problems/

O'Keefe, J. (2016, January 18). *10 ways you can advocate for your child with a learning disability*. Protectedtomorrows.com. https://protectedtomorrows.com/blog/2016/01/18/10-ways-you-can-advocate-your-child-learning-disability/

Parenting children with special needs. (n.d.). Www.bu.edu. https://www.bu.edu/wellness/social-well-being/parenting/parenting-children-with-special-needs/

Pinhorn, L. (2018, September 19). *Raising exceptional families with special needs children*. The Gottman Institute; The Gottman Institute. https://www.gottman.com/blog/raising-exceptional-families-with-special-needs-children/

Smith, S. L. (2002). What do parents of children with learning disabilities, ADHD, and related disorders deal with? *Pediatric Nursing, 28*(3), 254–257. https://pubmed.ncbi.nlm.nih.gov/12087645/

Success at school vs. success in life. (2016, March 23). The School of Life Articles. https://www.theschooloflife.com/thebookoflife/success-at-school-vs-success-in-life/

Taderera, C., & Hall, H. (2017). Challenges faced by parents of children with learning disabilities in opuwo, namibia. *African Journal of Disability*, *6*(0). https://doi.org/10.4102/ajod.v6i0.283

The impact of learning disabilities on social skills. (n.d.). LDRFA. https://www.ldrfa.org/impact-of-learning-disabilities-on-social-skills/

Turton, M. (2013, September 5). *What is neuroplasticity?* Www.getyourbreakthrough.com. http://www.getyourbreakthrough.com/blog/bid/310687/What-is-neuroplasticity

Understood Team. (n.d.). *Learning disabilities by the numbers.* Understood. https://www.understood.org/articles/en/learning-disabilities-by-the-numbers

Wilson, M. (2021, June 7). *Does Bill Gates have dyslexia?* Restaurant Norman. https://www.restaurantnorman.com/does-bill-gates-have-dyslexia/

Wright, P. W. D., & Wright, P. D. (2017). *Wrightslaw : From emotions to advocacy : The special education survival guide.* Harbor House Law Press.

www.ingramcontent.com/pod-product-compliance
Lightning Source LLC
LaVergne TN
LVHW051018080826
845145LV00009B/2688

* 9 7 8 1 9 5 6 0 1 8 2 7 1 *